ENJOY THE THRILL OF TRUE JOY AND HAPPINESS

THY WILL

BE DONE

JAMES KUCZYKOWSKI

ISBN 978-1-63961-751-7 (paperback)
ISBN 978-1-63961-752-4 (digital)

Christian Faith Publishing, Inc.
832 Park Avenue
Meadville, PA 16335
www.christianfaithpublishing.com

All Scripture quotations in this book are taken from the Catholic translation of the New American Bible, St. Joseph Edition.

Printed in the United States of America

Contents

Chapter 1

God's Will Is Love

Father, if thou art willing, remove this cup from
me; yet not my will but thine be done.

—Luke 22:42

From this prayer of Jesus Christ in the garden of Gethsemane on
the eve of his passion and death on a cross, humanity can arrive
at no other conclusion than there is nothing greater than God's will
for man.

Every word spoken by Jesus Christ has no other source than
love and has no other purpose than to express his love. It's all about
love.

Most people I know and perhaps even you, dear reader, say
many times each day the words "Thy will be done" in prayer; but do
we honestly desire and trust in God's will above ours? In my own life,
from the moment I started to sincerely and earnestly pray for God's
will above my own, a spirit of peace and joy began to penetrate my
soul, and so I would like in this book to share this joy and help others
enter it.

The Father's loving will for all mankind, in general, can be summed up with just one Word. That one Word has the name of Jesus Christ, God Incarnate.

> For God so loved the world that he gave
> his only Son so that whosoever believes in him
> may not perish, but might have eternal life. (John
> 3:16)

In an act of unmerited love, humanity is given by God our Savior and our loving Redeemer, whom the passage of John 3:16 speaks of, who paid a debt He did not owe because you and I owed a debt we could not pay.

John 3:16 is without any doubt the most popular Gospel verse known, but I like to focus on the verse that follows: "For God did not send his Son into the world to condemn the world, but that the world might be saved through him"(John 3:17).

This is the good news that Jesus gives to us all. It is that verse that for me contains the full richness and thickness of Jesus Christ's gospel message of joy, which we will attempt to journey toward in the pages that follow.

It is our heavenly Father's will for every human soul to have supreme joy here on earth and, someday, in heaven forever. And this is accomplished by the power and action of the Holy Spirit through his beloved Son, Jesus of Nazareth, the Christ.

God desires to send each of us our heart's desire so long as our desire conforms to his divine will and does not interfere with the sanctification of our immortal soul.

In this book, we will pray; and when we do, we will address God as Father because this is how Jesus Christ taught us to pray, what our relationship to God is, and what our relationship to each other is. We are all brothers and sisters in the one universal family of God. Yellow people, Red people, Black, and White—it does not matter. We are all made of earth, in the image of God, and after God's likeness. And to the earth we shall one day return.

We shall pray in the mighty name of Jesus Christ because Jesus Christ promises to give whatever we ask him or the Father in his name: "If you ask anything of me in my name, I will do it" (John 14:14) and "Whatever you ask the Father in my name, he will give you" (John 16:23). Wow! I'm all in! How about you, dear reader?

And we shall implore God to send the Holy Spirit upon us because without the Holy Spirit, we are handicapped and can do nothing worthwhile but with the Holy Spirit, we can do all things effortlessly and to good satisfaction. And we shall call on the Virgin Mary to pray with us and for us because she is an unfailing intercessor for all our petitions and made by her Son, Jesus Christ, the dispenser of all divine grace.

Jesus is likely to not ever deny his Mother anything as it was only through the Virgin Mary that Jesus came to be.

There is absolutely nothing that a man or woman could do that could cause an increase in Jesus Christ's love for him or her, and there is absolutely nothing any man or woman could do that could cause a decrease in his love for him or her. Jesus Christ's love for every human being is 100 percent perfect and unchangeable.

The fierce love of Jesus Christ for you and for me, no human tongue can declare. But the Holy Spirit can and does declare through the prophet Isaiah:

> It was our infirmities that he bore, our sufferings that he endured. He was pierced for our offenses, crushed for our sins, upon him was the chastisement that makes us whole, by his stripes we were healed. We had all gone astray like sheep, each following his own way; but the Lord laid upon him the guilt of us all.(Isaiah 53:4–6)

Prayer: "I love you, Christ Jesus, with all my heart and above all else. I acknowledge that I have sinned. I turn away from my sinful ways and turn to you, trusting in your infinite mercy. Breathe upon my soul your Holy Spirit. Be my Lord and God, my Savior and Master. Amen."

Understand that all mortal souls will tire more quickly from asking from Jesus than Jesus desires to give, for Jesus is infinite goodness all the time. His goodness is far beyond limited human comprehension and can bring good out of even the worst circumstances of life for nothing is beyond God's power, and "we know all things work together for good, for those who love God, who are called according to his purpose" (Romans 8:28).

I experienced this truth in my own life when at the young age of forty-eight I suffered a massive stroke that left me partially paralyzed and confined to a wheelchair in a nursing home for seven months (Carriage Inn of Steubenville, room 222), indeed a blessing in disguise. God often works in mysterious ways, and his blessings often arrive disguised as misfortune.

What was thought from the start of my illness as the worst thing that could ever happen has become my greatest blessing.

My stroke was a time of terrifying darkness, and I was feeling abandoned by God with nowhere to run and nowhere to hide as someone placed in prison without food or water. I felt so alone.

But turning to God was truly my only hope, and that I was able to do only with the help of a parish priest and many other friends from the twelve-step Anonymous fellowship, of which I am a grateful sober member.

I shared with Father my thoughts of God appearing distant and far away off. I remember, like it was this morning, Father sharing with me that "when God seems distant, that is precisely when he is most near." Father also encouraged recourse to the Virgin Mary and suggested we go to Mary, and so together, we prayed the Memorare. It is a prayer to the Virgin Mary that asks her to pray for us and is a statement of confidence in her all-powerful and never-known-to-fail prayerful intercession.

A very brief summary as to why I go and pray to the Virgin Mary when I most certainly can go straight to Jesus Christ is given in the final chapter of this little humble book.

God bless you!

Chapter 2

Beggars before God

But when you pray, go to your inner room, close
the door, and pray to your Father in secret. And
your Father who sees in secret will repay you.

—Matthew 6:6

What food and water are for the body, so prayer is for the soul. The human body in all its magnificence is limited and comprises a limited number of days, whereas the soul is unlimited and will last forever.

It is very awkward that as an almost global practice, many men and women place as a matter of first importance the nourishment of their bodies and have very little or no concern for the welfare of their soul. It just doesn't make sense!

I have titled this chapter on prayer "Beggars before God" because that is precisely what every human person is.

From the most financially liquid to the least financially liquid and everyone in between, we are all beggars before God.

You may say, "I'm not a beggar before God. I worked hard for all I have." That may be true, and there is no doubt that you have labored much for all you have or you inherited wealth, but God has given you the ability to work or was seeing to your fortune anonymously behind the scenes and can remove one's good health or good fortune in the blink of an eye.

With that thought, let us recall the words of John the Baptist: "No one can receive anything except what comes from heaven" (John 3:27).

Now there can be no greater or wiser person to go to for guidance on how to pray than Jesus Christ, Wisdom Incarnate, as his wisdom is far superior to the wisdom of all saints, philosophers, and theologians of human history put together.

The Lord's Prayer that Jesus taught is the all-time perfect prayer—first of all because of its Author and, second, drawing from St. Thomas Aquinas: "In the Lord's Prayer, we not only pray for the things that we should pray for but in the precise order in which we should pray for them."

So at our Savior's command and formed by divine teaching, we dare to say: "Our Father who art in heaven, hallowed be thy name. Thy kingdom come; *thy will be done* on earth as it is in heaven. Give us today our daily bread and forgive us our trespasses *as* we have forgiven those who trespass against us; and lead us not into temptation, but deliver us from the evil one. Amen."

Also, in his Sermon on the Mount, the Lord Jesus gives a very simple guide to effective prayer, which can easily be brought to mind by remembering the acronym "ASK":

> Ask, and it will be given to you; seek and
> you will find; knock and the door will be opened
> to you. (Matthew 7:7)

When praying preset common prayers such as the Lord's Prayer or Hail Mary, it is important to say the words very slowly, pondering well over each word that is said.

Before beginning prayer, it is right and just to say a prayer to the Holy Spirit, to acknowledge God's supreme dominion over all people and man's absolute dependence upon him for everything.

There was once one young lad however who did not know this truth, so he asked his father to teach him how to pray. The young lad's father took his son to the nearest pool of water and very lovingly grabbed him by the back of the neck and dunked him in the water: The boy began to struggle and fight for air and finally came up out of the water. Then his father said to him, "Son, when you desire to pray as much as you desired to breathe air, no one will have to teach you how to pray."

Prayer, simply put, is having a conversation with God and is man's most effective communication line to God.

Just as important as it is for prayer to accompany the reading of scripture, so also it is vitally important that the reading of scripture always accompanies prayer. God certainly speaks to us through others, but most especially, God speaks to us through the inspired Word of God.

Sacred Scripture has the answers to man's deepest questions and most burdensome problems. So it is true wisdom to become familiar with the scriptures just as we become familiar with the people we love.

When a man and woman fall in love, oftentimes, they want to spend as much time as possible together, and that is exactly how it is for those who desire to have intimate friendship with God.

By spending time in scripture, a person's love for God is nourished and strengthened, so the prayerful reading of scripture should be considered number one on each person's to-do list each day.

Noteworthy of mention here is the ancient method of reading scripture known as *Lectio Divina* and the daily recitation of the Holy Rosary. Both of them are beyond the scope of this little simple book. But a little research on your part, dear reader, will prove quite fruitful.

There is a principle at work when we pray, and that principle is *Whatever the heart of man believes, the power of God achieves*. Nothing is impossible for God, and actually, nothing is impossible for one who believes as Jesus Christ himself said, "All things are possible to him who believes"(Mark 9:23).

Seven straight days without prayer makes one weak, so take the time to pray—it is the greatest power on earth.

Everybody who desires a meaningful prayer life should consider starting their prayer time with a prayer to the Holy Spirit. Adapted from Veni Creator, I invite you, dear reader, to pray with me the following prayer to the Holy Spirit:

> Come, Creator Spirit Blest. And in the depths of my soul, take up thy rest. Come upon me with all thy possible grace and all thy possible heavenly aid and set on fire this heart and soul, which you have made. Kindle my senses from heaven above and let it be that my whole being be constantly filled and overflowing with all thy joy, with all thy peace, and with all thy love. With all thy gifts and firm and all thy gifts and fruits high, the great weakness of my flesh supply. Amen!

Now there once was a young man who was conversing with the Lord and said to him, "Lord God, isn't it true that to you, one day is like a thousand years and a thousand years like one day and that one million dollars is like just one dollar to you and one dollar to you is the same as a million?"

And the Lord God replied, "Yes, son, this is true."

Then the young man said to the Lord, "Then will you please give me one million dollars since to you, it would only be like giving me just one dollar?"

Then the Lord God said, "Okay, but give me a day or so to come up with the cash."

Yes. God hears and answers all our prayers but in his time, not ours, and in a way not foreseen by man. And sometimes, God's answer is "no" only because he has a better plan.

One of the most powerful mantra prayers that can be prayed, though, for any intention is the simple repetition of the Holy Name of Jesus.

Why? Because the Holy Name of Jesus is truthfully a treasury of the very highest degree for within it lies hidden the full infinite power of Almighty God.

It was by the holy name of Jesus that the twelve apostles worked all their deeds of marvel, and it was by the holy name of Jesus that the rigid Roman Empire in the first century was converted to the new Christian religion of love and brotherhood.

Whenever facing rough and tough circumstances that are sure to come, simply repeat continually the Holy Name of Jesus or St. Paul's words—"I can do all things through Christ who strengthens me"—and experience for yourself the things that God enables you to accomplish.

Humanity would do well in this twenty-first century by calling on the holy name of Jesus asking him to put an end to this current coronavirus pandemic.

Saint Augustine said, "Pray as if everything depended on God and work as if everything depended on you." Work and pray vigorously, yes, but be sure to leave the results in the care of God (results are God's department).

Even so, attaining our desires and goals through prayer is not only scriptural but, according to some sources, is scientifically sound based on how the subconscious mind works.

Scriptural because "what the wicked man fears will befall him but the desires of the just will be granted" (Proverbs 10:24).

And scientifically sound because of how the human mind works. That is, as I recollect, the subconscious is an obedient servant of the whole human mind that follows the commands given to it and makes a person's behavior consistent with their emotionalized thoughts and desires.

So whatever occupies the human mind is sure to fall upon them as the above passage from the book of Proverbs instructs. So be sure to fill your mind only with positive emotions such as love, peace, and joy as well as happiness and gratitude.

The greatest men and women of human history employed prayer constantly and changed the world for the better. Prayer worked for them because they earnestly prayed in a way that was pleasing and acceptable to God Most High, in a way that was free of selfish and sinful motives.

There is no great hidden secret to acquiring answers to prayer. The condition of receiving lies in first of all God's will and, second, the character trait of believing that what is being prayed for is already in the possession of the one praying without having even a glimmer of doubt.

Jesus Christ himself said: "Truly I tell you, if you have faith as small as a mustard seed, you can say to this mountain, 'Move from here to there'; and it will move. Nothing will be impossible for you" (Matthew 17:20).

One way to look at prayer is to think of it as a personal business meeting with God.

Some questions that can be asked in this meeting to determine if your will lies within the boundaries of God's will are as follows: (1) Is what I am about to do or say pleasing to God? (2) Is what I am about to do or say the right thing to do or say? (3) Is what I am about to do or say the beautiful thing to do or say? (4) Will what I am about to do or say benefit my fellow man?

If we can answer "yes" to those four questions, then we can be pretty sure that we are well conformed to God's will and walk on secure ground.

Prayer of surrender to God's will: "Merciful Father, I entrust all my concerns into your care, merging my human will with your divine will, so I pray not for my intentions but for your will to be done always and everywhere and in all circumstances and in every aspect of being. Amen."

Now there once was a man who was praying for potatoes when behold, suddenly, he heard a voice from heaven that said: "Get a hoe and start digging."

God will do for us what we can't do for ourselves, but God will not do for us what we can do for ourselves.

He may not always give us what we want, but always God gives us what we need, and he gives what we need at the precise time that we need it most.

May God's face shine upon you!

Chapter 3

Drop the Resentments

"Vengeance is mine!" says the Lord.

"Blessed are the merciful for they will obtain mercy" (Matthew 5:7) are just a few of the immortal words of Jesus Christ regarding anger.

And one of the best reasons for letting go of resentments is "judgement is merciless to one who has not shown mercy" (James 2:13).

We have just two options:

1. Be merciful as our heavenly Father is merciful.
2. Count ourselves among the damned. There is no third option.

The frightful thing about harboring resentment is that when we have resentment (just or unjust), we will find ourselves harboring anger toward Jesus Christ himself for he said: "Whatsoever you do to the least of my brethren, you do for me" (Matthew 25:40).

All mankind is called to remember well and echo his words while still hanging upon his cross: "Father, forgive them, for they do not know what they are doing."

Be sure of this: no human person has the power to make another person angry. It is anger already dwelling in a man that is squeezed out of him. Other people only remind us of our anger within, and so we let ourselves fall into a state of uncalled-for bitter resentful anger.

This anger is like lemon juice. When I squeeze a lemon, what pours from the lemon is lemon juice; and when I squeeze a person full of anger, what shows up is their anger.

One of the major reasons that I get all twisted and bent out of shape in this way is because I, all too often, am much too concerned over the passing joys and satisfactions of earth and incorrectly feel cheated. But if I can rid myself of the desire of passing things, then I leave more room in my soul for the joys of the Holy Spirit to come upon me.

So what is one to do?

I am a member of a fellowship of men and women that encourages its members to pray for the welfare and well-being of the people whom they are angry with.

A common prayer that is prayed to eliminate resentment is a prayer that, for our purposes, will be labeled henceforth as the "Compassion Prayer."

The Compassion Prayer: "Dear God, give to (name of person resented) all the abundance and happiness that is possible to a human soul living on this earth, in time and, someday, in heaven forever. Amen."

Resentment is nothing other than hoping for a better past and is as senseless as drinking a glass of poison, sitting down, and waiting for that other person to get sick and die.

The only person resentment can harm is the one who has it, and bearing this form of hatred is like a storm that has the power to destroy, even kill (not that other person but the one who resents).

If a person's relationship with God is right and their basic instincts of life are not out of control, then a man or woman can live joyfully in just about any circumstance that comes upon him or her.

Being resentful, justified or unjustified, is the negative of negatives because it brings upon man waves of negativity and, worst of all, blocks a person off from the spirit of God. Oh, horror of horrors!

The one thing that has helped most in freeing myself of resentment is praying for those whom I was feeling resentful toward, asking

God to give them all the abundance and happiness that is possible for a human soul. My first twelve-step sponsor, Mark M., shared with me that if I have resentment that I want to be free from, if I would pray for that person every day for two weeks a prayer such as the Compassion Prayer, I would be set free of that particular resentment. And where I had bitter anger toward a person, I would begin to have an attitude of compassion and love for the person whom I was once angry with.

Resentment is a negative emotion that does nothing but bring about more negativity and drain a person of all their energy.

So let's get started with the building of a resentment-free heart by listing two or three people whom that we find hard to forgive and pray the Compassion Prayer for each of them.

I am resentful toward

1. _____
2. _____
3. _____

Now, I need to locate a notebook that can be used exclusively for this purpose and begin writing down in this book all the names of people I have a problem with and pray the Compassion Prayer for each of them. Praying for others, second only to laying down one's life for one's friends, is the greatest and most rewarding act of love that one person can do for another.

Later, whenever the slightest spark of ill feeling for a person rises in my heart, I must stop whatever I am doing, get out a pen or pencil and my resentment book, and start writing down names and begin praying the Compassion Prayer for each of the persons whom I have listed.

Afterward, I may wish to consider praying the Compassion Prayer for all those who cross my path every day.

If you follow this suggestion, dear reader, little by little, the joy of living is sure to be yours.

God bless you.

Chapter 4

Gratitude

Give thanks to the Lord, for he is good.
His love endures forever.

—Psalm 136

Gratitude is what I call a magnetic multiplier. The greater the gratitude a man has, the more God gives to him to be grateful for. And it is much more than just being thankful for what one has.

It is expressed in doing works of mercy, the most perfect being patiently bearing injuries done to us and praying for others.

It is right and just always and everywhere and in all circumstances to give thanks to God, the Almighty Father, who from the rising of the sun to its setting bestows on the world all that is good.

Gratitude is a choice and is the very finest of all human emotions. It is the best medicine known to man as it heals the whole person and indeed is the foundation of all achievement and abundance.

If we have not all the things we want, let us be grateful for the things that we do not have that we wouldn't want such as cancer or heart disease.

When a person sincerely desires to live in communion with God's will, then cultivating an attitude of gratitude should be considered as indispensable.

There are as many benefits in having a grateful heart as there are stars in the heavens. To follow are just a few.

Gratitude makes a person happier and eliminates stress. It improves sleep and enhances self-esteem—some pretty good reasons to begin right away!

The first thing we want to do to develop this character trait is to pray the Gratitude Prayer every day twice a day—once in the morning and once before going to sleep. It takes only a minute but will most certainly produce bountiful fruit.

The Gratitude Prayer: "Dear God, I thank you for everybody and everything that you have given me. I thank you for everybody and everything that you have taken away from me. I thank you for everybody and everything that you have left me. I thank you for everybody and everything that you did not permit me to have. Amen."

Next, we want to begin a gratitude list. "Count your blessings," my dear mother, Dorothy, used to say. It is best to locate a place in the notebook that can be used exclusively for this purpose.

To get started on the list, we will try our best to think of two or three people or things that we are most thankful for. Write them down on the gratitude space. If number 1 is not Jesus Christ, then I gently suggest that one has a lot of soul-searching to do.

Once you have the names down on paper, begin praying the Compassion Prayer for each person listed. It is best to add to this list every day and review it from time to time every month.

As our list grows larger, God on his part will send us more and more to be placed on our list. It's a pretty good deal!

Cultivating an attitude of gratitude is so important that I am urging all my readers to begin with their gratitude list right away.

But before we begin this exercise, I would like to share with you a short story of a young man who thought he had nothing to be grateful for.

There was once a young lad who complained to God because he thought he didn't have anything to be grateful for, explaining he didn't even have enough money to pay back those from whom he borrowed money.

God replied, "Could you not, then, be grateful that you are not one of those from whom you borrowed the money?"

That silly story demonstrates the truth that there is always something to be thankful for.

Whenever I tell that story, I am always reminded of the man who was complaining about needing a new pair of shoes when simultaneously he saw a man with no feet.

God will always place along our path exactly who we need at every given moment. For instance, when I was in the nursing home, I was praying to God asking him with a deep sigh if I'd ever walk normally again. And right at that moment, I glanced across the hall into the room of one of the other residents, and what did I see was a man who had no legs.

No matter how grievous our circumstances, there is always someone in the world who has it worse.

Now I can talk about being grateful all I want, but if my gratitude is not proven by what I do for my fellow man, then my gratitude is mere talk and not pleasing nor acceptable in the eyes of God.

Gratitude is an action word, so let's get started with the gratitude list.

Gratitude List

I am most thankful for

1. _____
2. _____
3. _____

Remember to pray the Compassion Prayer for each person on your list, right now and every day.

God will most certainly bless you when you do without you even knowing it. You'll see.

God bless you.

Chapter 5

Generosity

Remember this: Whoever sows sparingly will also
reap sparingly. Each of you should give what you have
decided in your heart to give, not reluctantly or under
compulsion, for God loves a cheerful giver.

—1 Corinthians 9:6–8

True generosity is the habit of giving or loving without expecting something in return.

When one gives or loves expecting something in return, that is barter, a business transaction, not love.

It is a paradox of this life that we only get to keep what we have by giving it away. Very odd but true!

The experience of many shows that people who give of their time, talent, or treasury, expecting nothing in return, experience greater joy than what comes to them by any other means, except by having a perpetual indwelling of the Holy Spirit.

Whatsoever we have is because God has given it, and we please him very much when we share his blessings with others. So it will go very well to establish a well-thought-out giving plan if you haven't already done so. This plan should be written on paper and read aloud each day.

If one's giving plan is not written, then that one does not have a giving plan but rather good intentions, and good intentions without action are almost always followed by more good intentions, and nothing is accomplished.

It is a spiritual law that the more one gives, the more is given to them. Knowing full well this spiritual law, Jesus Christ said: "Give, and it shall be given unto you" (Luke 6:38).

And the greatest act of generosity that one can express toward one's fellow man, second only to laying down one's life for one's friends, is not with the pocketbook but by praying for others, even our enemies and those who have harmed us.

We often hear that "God will never be outdone in generosity."

And though that is true, God strongly encourages man to imitate his generosity and promises handsome rewards for doing so. The one area that God permits testing him is given in the area of giving:

> "Bring the whole tithe into the storehouse,
> that there may be food in my house, and try me
> in this," says the Lord of Hosts: "Shall I not open
> for you the floodgates of heaven, to pour down
> blessing upon you without measure?" (Malachi
> 3:10)

Mother Mary Angelica, founder of the Eternal Word Television Network (EWTN), said frequently on her television program, "We are all called to be great saints. Don't miss the opportunity."

Drawing on her thought, I say to you, dear readers, that every human soul is called to be a channel of God's greatest attributes of love and mercy and God will send us many opportunities each day. Don't miss your opportunities!

The benefits of generosity are beautifully expressed in the book of Proverbs: "Honor the Lord with your wealth, with first fruits of all your produce; then will your barns be filled with grain, with new wine your vats will overflow" (Proverbs 3:9–10).

God's gift to a human soul is more talent and ability than what one could ever wish to use in their lifetime, and man's gift back to God is to develop his gift and to share it with others.

A person's generosity is nothing less than satisfying the twofold commandment of loving God and neighbor and will always return to the giver multiplied many times over for it is true that "God will never be outdone in generosity."

And finally, Jesus Christ himself commands: "Give to everyone who asks of you and from the one who takes what is yours do not demand it back" (Luke 6:30).

"Give and give and give and give some more!" is what my dear mother, Dorothy, used to say.

Prayer: "Lord, teach me to be generous. Teach me to serve you as you deserve, to give and not count the cost, to fight and not heed the wounds, to toil and not seek for rest, to labor and not seek reward, except to know that I am doing your will. Amen" (St. Ignatius of Loyola, 1491–1556).

Chapter 6

Trust in God

Blessed is the man who trusts in the
Lord, whose hope is the Lord.

—Jeremiah 17:7

While beginning to write this chapter, what came in the mail was a letter sent to me by the Salesian Missions, a very worthy cause to add to your giving plan should you be in search of one.

In this letter was a reflection card on trusting in God by St. Francis De Sales as follows:

> The same everlasting Father who cares for you today will care for you tomorrow and every day. Either he will shield you from suffering or give you strength to bear it. Be at peace then and put aside all anxious thoughts and imaginings.

Although it can be forgotten or even outright rejected, it seems to me, and others, that each human person is given at birth a natural human instinct of trusting in God as the popular quote from St. Augustine suggests as I remember it: "Thou hast made us for thyself, O Lord, and our heart is restless until it finds its rest in you."

Trusting in God is nourished and strengthened when a person acknowledges God's supreme dominion over all things and concedes to man's absolute dependence upon God for everything.

Oftentimes we have to get out of our comfort zone and let God be God; but too often, all of us including the writer want to hold on to what we know, even misery, because there is a peculiar comfort in what we know and a seemingly real fear of the unknown—thus the slogan "Let go, let God." People nowadays even take comfort in a neurotic way in things that do not concern them.

Trusting in God, like all other admirable attributes of man, is a process; and the beginning of this particular process is prayer and doing small initial leaps of faith.

Faith, by the way, is said to be an acronym for "Fantastic Adventure in Trusting Him." And as we begin to receive more and more confidence in God by making consecutive small leaps of faith with the smaller circumstances that fall to our share, little by little, our trust in God increases; and as our trust in God increases, so does our joy in life. Then by the grace of God we eventually become equipped to make larger leaps of faith as "God does not call the equipped but equips the called." It is important to have patience and let God be God. To live life on God's terms and in God's time for patience obtains all things.

The Holy Bible is saturated with passages encouraging trust in God. We will take a brief look at a few that are in the book of Psalms and in the book of Proverbs. In the book of Psalms, we find the awesome words of Psalm 23: "The Lord is my shepherd, I shall not want." The book of Proverbs instructs us to "trust in the Lord with all your heart, on your own intelligence do not rely. In all your ways be mindful of him, and he will make straight your paths" (Proverbs 3:5–6).

Finding passages in the Holy Bible that encourage man to trust in God is like trying to find water in the sea. One doesn't have to labor much. Just open your Bible and start reading. In particular, the Psalms have been a major source of trust in God for centuries and the book of Proverbs likewise. Notice that the word *trust* spells *us*, so we are not walking alone, but we are each day walking with the living God.

Perhaps the greatest obstacle to trusting in God is man's spirit of rebellion and his false pride, which makes him incapable of letting life happen in God's time and on God's terms.

One way of establishing or reestablishing trust in God is by man's complete acceptance of and total surrender to God's will in all things and all circumstances and every aspect of being.

A short but powerful prayer noteworthy of mention here is an act of surrender to God's will.

Prayer: "Heavenly Father and God of mercy, in the name of Jesus, I place all my concerns into your care, merging my human will with your most loving divine will. Amen."

I would like to share here the poem "Footprints in the Sand," a poem that I received from my father during US Air Force Basic Training that has had an impact on me some forty years later.

Footprints in the Sand

A certain man had a dream one night, and in his dream, he saw his entire life in an instant. He saw himself walking along a sandy beach with the Lord Jesus and saw before him two sets of footprints: one his and the other the Lord's. When life was going well for him, he noticed two sets of footprints; but when life became troublesome, he saw only one set of footprints.

So he questioned the Lord about this, saying, "Why, Lord, at the tough and rough times of my life, did you leave me to walk alone?"

The Lord replied, wearing a meek and humble smile, "My child, my child, my child, I love you with a love surpassing all love and will never forsake or abandon you. You see, those times when you saw only one set of footprints, it was then that I carried you."

And so we come to one of the most comforting passages of Sacred Scripture that recalls Jesus Christ's words to his disciples, "It is I. Do not be afraid."

God bless you!

Chapter 7

Do Not Be Afraid

Fear not, I am with you; be not dismayed;
I am your God. I will strengthen you.
And uphold you with my right hand of justice.

—Isaiah 41:10

The words "Do not be afraid" are recorded in Sacred Scripture 365 times, once for every day of the year. What is your opinion, dear reader? Could it be possible that God is trying to communicate something to us mortals here?

The words of Jesus—"Take courage. Do not be afraid. It is I"—are words spoken for people of every generation in every nation under heaven until the end of time.

Proverbs tells us what a man fears will fall upon him: "What the wicked man fears will befall him but the desires of the just will be granted" (Proverbs 10:24). This is perhaps why the words "Do not be afraid" are recorded in Scripture so frequently.

There are no accidents or mistakes in God's world. Everything is exactly the way it is supposed to be, and time is passing according to God's loving will.

God Most High is in absolute control of everything and every person although sometimes it seems quite the opposite.

God is in charge, and that's the way it is!

You may ask, "What about accidental death?" Remember this: God never takes away life. He only changes it into something much greater than what the limited human mind can comprehend or even imagine.

We are peculiar beings. We even at times try to counsel God and advise him on what is best for us. But God needs no human counsel. He knows everything well.

The hand of God is everywhere and has been since the beginning of time and will never cease to be.

St. Teresa of Avila, who lived in the sixteenth century and was proclaimed a doctor of the church for her writings, said: "Let nothing disturb you. Let nothing frighten you. All things are passing away: God never changes. Patience obtains all things. Whoever has God lacks for nothing; God alone suffices."

Four centuries later, following the same thought, St. Padre Pio of Pietrelcina said: "Pray, hope, and don't worry!"

The reason people have fear is self-reliance utterly falls short and people fail to recognize and acknowledge the truth of God's supreme dominion over all things and all people.

And truth is not an idea or philosophy but a person, the person of Jesus Christ who said: "I am the way, the truth and the life." Without the way, there is no going; without the truth, there is no knowing; and without the life, there is no living.

We often hear "one is no fool to let go of what one cannot keep in order to keep what one cannot lose." So let it be our firm resolution to let go of anything that hinders our being conformed to God's will.

When letting go and letting God becomes our only alternative and we hold on to any idea of how God ought to handle things, we haven't turned anything over to God but are trying to be God ourselves. And that way of thinking just doesn't work. By all means, make plans and work hard toward accomplishing them but leave the results to God because results are God's department, not man's.

All people everywhere are called to have total dependence upon God with good reason. Man almost always finds the blessings that come to him when he places himself under the care and direction of God far exceed what comes to him by any other way.

This is seen continuously in an Anonymous twelve-step fellow-ship group, Alcoholics Anonymous, for example. A new man will come to the fellowship, obtain a sponsor and home group, begin working the twelve steps, turn his will and life over to God as he understands God…and almost at once, miraculously, a tremendous turn of circumstances begin to be showered upon the man without measure. Coincidence?

I think not! There are no coincidences in God's world. Truly, there is something to the act of abandoning oneself to God.

Prayer: "Heavenly Father and God of love and mercy, I place all my cares and concerns into your hands, merging my human will completely to your divine will. May your will be done in me and through me always. Amen."

God bless you!

Chapter 8

Take Up Thy Cross

Consider it all joy, my brothers, when you encounter various trials, for you know that the testing of your faith produces perseverance. And let perseverance be perfect, so that you may be perfect and complete lacking in nothing.

—James 1:2–4

There are a few things I can assure you, dear reader:

a. We do not know with certainty what tomorrow will bring, not even our weather forecasts are 100 percent accurate.
b. We all have a cross to carry.
c. The way I carry my cross will largely determine my eternal destiny.

As long as we live in this world, no human person can be without a cross.

The royal road of the cross is the road that the King of kings walked, and it is the road that his subjects must also walk. There is no way of going around it. We can only pray for the grace to endure it. And when our certain crosses do arrive, know it is through the cross that a man is humbled and by the power of the Holy Spirit, triumphantly sanctified, prepared for an eternal dwelling, and given the true joy of God, a joy that has no limits.

I don't know you personally, dear reader, but there is one thing very personal about you that I do know. That is that we have an absolute share in Jesus Christ's passion and death upon his cross. Perhaps our share is many crosses, and perhaps our crosses seem too heavy to bear. But be of good cheer because God will never give more than we can handle and will always give the needed strength to endure all pain and suffering. By sharing in the passion and cross of our dear Savior, we are also given to share in his joy of resurrection. Oftentimes, many of us ask, "Why this cross, Lord? Why not some other cross?"

However, if we could see all the crosses of humanity piled up, we would beg God for the one that is ours. There is always someone who has it worse.

We all have a cross to carry, but our dear Savior is with us as Jesus himself promised: "I am with you always even to the end of the world" (Matthew 28:20).

If I am in a state of pain and suffering today, I should know that I do not suffer alone. Jesus Christ is at my side, crucified with me and in me just as surely as he was crucified on the way to Calvary. And I should know that my pain and suffering when united to his contributes to the redemption of many souls. This is what the Catholic Church calls redemptive suffering, primarily based on St. Paul's letter to the first-century Christians at Colossae: "Now I rejoice in my sufferings for your sake, and in my flesh I am filling up what is lacking in the afflictions of Christ on behalf of his body, which is the church" (Colossians 1:24).

Prayer: "Heavenly Father, I unite myself to the pain and suffering of your divine Son, Jesus. Thus, united, I offer to you my life, with all the aches and pains that accompany it for your will to be accomplished in me and through me always and everywhere in all circumstances and every aspect of my being. Amen."

St. Therese of Lisieux expresses the acceptance of Christ's invitation to share in his passion very profoundly in her Act of Oblation to Merciful Love, which follows with minor adaptions:

> Lord Jesus, to make a single act of perfect love, I offer myself as a victim soul to your merciful love, O my God, asking you to consume me incessantly allowing all your graces to fill my soul to overflowing that I may be a martyr of your love. May this martyrdom cause my soul, after having prepared to appear before you, take its flight without any delay into the eternal embrace of your infinite merciful love. Amen.

God bless you always!

Chapter 9

One Day at a Time

Do not worry about tomorrow; tomorrow will take care of itself.

—Matthew 6:34

Tomorrow is promised to no one, and we are all living on borrowed time. "Yesterday is history, tomorrow is a mystery, all we have is today, and truly all we truly have is the present moment."

One very fruitful way to live in the present is to walk in the presence of God.

So with all care and diligence give every task undivided attention by doing every task with God and for the love of God and for his greater glory.

My dad was a carpenter, and he tried his very best to teach us kids to live rightly in the present moment by telling us quite often, "Do things right the first time. Then you won't have to go back to fix things or clean things up."

Another very helpful way to living one day at a time is to adopt a set of principles or rules to live by. To follow is a list that you may wish to consider:

1. The day begins at six, so let us set our alarms for five. This allows time to get cleaned up and eat breakfast before we begin our day.

2. Be no man's rival but every man's friend.
3. Put no man down but only lift high Jesus Christ.
4. Live by the golden rule: "Do unto others whatsoever you want them to do to you."
5. Recite aloud every day Christ's Sermon on the Mount.
6. Count your blessings.
7. Begin and end each day with a prayer of praising God and thanking him for his always infinite goodness.

A prayer that is very dear to my heart and very useful to living joyfully is the full version of the Serenity Prayer. There is much debate over the original author, so proper credit cannot be given here.

The Serenity Prayer (full version): "God, grant me the serenity to accept the things I cannot change, courage to change the things I can, and the wisdom to know the difference. Living one day at a time, enjoying one moment at a time, accepting hardship as the pathway to peace. Taking as he did this sinful world as it is, not as I would have it. Trusting that he will make all things right if I surrender to his will. That I may be reasonably happy in this life and supremely happy with him forever in the next. Amen."

This prayer reminds us that very often we need to make changes in our lives. "If we keep on doing what we've always done, we will keep on getting what we have always got!"

Perhaps the greatest obstacle to enjoying the present day is the constant desire to know what is coming tomorrow, but tomorrow is not ours to see, nor is it promised to anyone. We are living on borrowed time.

Another key ingredient to joyful living is letting go of the things that are not our concern.

For example, there were two Irish monks, Brian and Sean, walking down a country road talking about the goodness that came their way from God. As they were walking, they came to a water stream and saw a beautiful woman crying because she could not get to the other side. So Brian put the woman on his shoulders and carried her across the stream. After making the crossing, Brian put the woman down, and the two monks continued on their journey.

They walked about a mile down the road, and Sean said to Brian, "Brian, you know well that although the spirit is willing, the flesh is weak. By placing that woman on your shoulders, you could have been enticed to the desires of the flesh."

Brian said to Sean in reply, "Brian, I let go of the woman after making the crossing. Why is it that you still hold on to her?"

God bless you!

Chapter 10

Let Go and Let God

In this chapter, I would like to bring to the surface and recall the surrender to God's will made by the Virgin Mary at the time of the angel Gabriel's announcement that she was to be the Mother of man's Blessed Redeemer. Without hesitation and with automatic death by stoning in front of her, she said yes to God's will by responding to the angel's message by saying, "Behold, the handmaid of the Lord, let it be done unto me according to your word" (Luke 1:38).

Although not everyone will be called to say yes to God's will as valiantly as the Virgin Mary, all of us will someday be challenged to make an act of surrender to God's providence.

Act of surrender to God Most High: "Heavenly Father, into your hands I commend my everything: all my hopes and dreams, all my cares and concerns, all my desires and aspirations, and my entire will and my whole life. Amen."

Many of us pray the words "Thy will be done" several times throughout the day, but do we desire God's will above ours?

That is, by the way, one of the secrets to joyful living, to earnestly desire God's will to be done always and everywhere in all circumstances and every aspect of being. And another secret is to let go of all preconceived ideas of how we think God ought to handle things and give God complete control.

God bless you always!

Chapter 11

Go to Mary

And Jesus saw his mother and the disciple standing by, whom
he loved. And he said to his mother, "Woman, behold, thy
son." Then he said to his disciple, "Behold, thy mother."
And from that hour the disciple took her into his home.

—John 19:26–27

In light of Jesus Christ's words from the cross right before expiring and the action of the beloved disciple from that hour, devotion to the Virgin Mary became completely logical and sensible as Jesus gifted to the human race the maternal protection of his Mother through the beloved disciple.

St. Louis-Marie de Montfort, in his prayer to Mary, said that "the Virgin Mary triumphs gloriously in heaven at the right hand of her Son and holds absolute sway over angels, men, and demons."

With that thought in mind, it should be known that every single prayer petition to God that passes through Mary's Immaculate Heart is made pure and acceptable.

The Virgin Mary obtains all we ask if what we ask for is compatible with God's will.

One might reasonably ask, "Why go to the Virgin Mary when I can go straight to Jesus?" That is a good question that has a very good answer.

While it is true that no emissary is needed to be received by Jesus Christ, it is equally true that Jesus Christ would never deny his Mother anything. So it behooves us all to ask Mary to intercede and pray for us as she is the unfailing intercessor given to us by Jesus Christ himself.

Even non-Catholic Christians are compelled by the force of truth to admit that the Virgin Mary is the giver of God's greatest blessing upon the human race, the incarnation of Christ. It was only through her flesh and blood that Jesus became our brother and Redeemer.

It is my sincere hope and prayer that all who read this book will begin to live joyfully and securely under the tender and loving protection of the Blessed Virgin Mary.

I would like it known for my separated brethren, as praiseworthy as your zeal for Jesus Christ is, the thinking that devotion to the Virgin Mary in some way takes away from the love of Jesus Christ is just not true. One's love for and devotion to the Virgin Mary makes more perfect one's love for Jesus Christ.

Indeed, the Virgin Mary is, St. Louis de Montfort taught, the shortest, quickest, and most secure way to touch the heart of her divine Son, Jesus Christ.

> The Lord bless you and keep you! The Lord let his face shine upon you and be gracious to you; The Lord look kindly upon you and give you peace. (Numbers 6:24–26)

About the Author

Little Jimmy K. is a Roman Catholic by faith and an honorably discharged veteran of the US Air Force. He lives a somewhat solitary lifestyle and resides in the small village of Wintersville, Ohio.

James has a joyful personality, and it is always pleasure to be in his company.

He is a man of prayer and has a contagious love for God, which can be felt in his joyful spirit. He prays the Rosary daily and regularly attends daily mass, which, he confesses, is the major cause to his happiness and joy.

CPSIA information can be obtained
at www.ICGtesting.com
Printed in the USA
BVHW092304051022
648789BV00002B/112

9 781639 617517